Have at You Now!

Have at You Now!

Poems by John Gery

CW Books

Published by CW Books
P.O. Box 541106
Cincinnati, OH 45254-1106

ISBN: 9781625490704
LCCN: 2014931116

Poetry Editor: Kevin Walzer
Business Editor: Lori Jareo

Visit us on the web at wwww.readcwbooks.com

Acknowledgments

The following poems have previously appeared elsewhere (sometimes in different versions). I wish to thank the editors of these publications for their support and for permission to republish the poems here.

Burlesque Press: "Bestial Oblivion" and "Your Other Woman"
Gulf Coast: "RE: Volition"
Interdisciplinary Humanities: "After a Poetry Reading, Delmore Schwartz Returns to His Hotel"
The Iowa Review: "Grief"
Journal of College Writing: "Done Reading," "In *Travesty*," and "This Latest Emptiness"
Journal of Southern Religion: "Enough, Enough"
Louisiana Literature: "Sunset at Kalemegdan"
Maple Leaf Rag III (Portals Press): "The Next Misstep"
Maple Leaf Rag IV (Portals Press): "The Obvious" and "Disaster"
New Orleans Review: "Seepage"
Nonforgotten (Japan): "After a Poetry Reading, Delmore Schwartz Returns to His Hotel"
Normal School: "On the Fly"
Pivot: "Lag Time" and "Country Matters: *Le Déjeuner sur L'herbe*"
Poet Lore: "For Biljana, Who Says the Older She Grows, the Less She Knows"
Prairie Schooner: "Acceptance, Finally" and "In Our Time"
Sendecki.com: "Part of a Sudden"
Smartish Pace: "The Reach"
Southern Poetry Anthology (Vol. IV): "Grace" and "What Are Eyes for?"
War, Literature, and the Arts: "To a Friend Dying of Cancer in a War Zone," "The Secret of Stealth," "Summit Summary," and "Spring Offensive"

"Grief," "When Nadine Gordimer Spoke,"and "English Is Dying" appear in Dzon Geri (John Gery), *Americki Duh: Izbrane Pesme* (*American Ghost: Selected Poems*), trans. into Serbian by Biljana D. Obradovic (Belgrade, Former Republic of Yugoslavia: Raska skola, 1999; Merrick, NY: Cross-Cultural Communications, 1999), ed. Bratislav Milanović (Belgrade) and Stanley H. Barkan (New York). "Spring Offensive" also appears in *Poets against the War*, ed. Sam Hamill with Sally Anderson and others (New York: Thunder's

Mouth/Nation Books, 2003). "Summit Summary" also appears (in Serbian, trans. by V. Bogdanovic) in *The Curse: Serbia, Spring 1999*, ed. Moma Dimic (Belgrade: Assoc. of Writers of Serbia, 1999) and is reprinted in *Ostaci Svetlasti: Stravi Pesnici (1964-2004) [Remnants of Light: Poets from Abroad (1964-2004)]*, ed. Moma Dimic (Belgrade: Assoc. of Writers of Serbia, 2005). "English Is Dying" was originally published in a limited edition as *Shaman Broadside* No. 28 (New Orleans: Trembling Pillow Press, 17 Aug. 1999), ed. David Brinks. "Miracoli" was originally published in *Gondola Signore Gondola: Venice in 20th Century American Poetry/Venezia nella Poesia Americana del Novecento* (English/Italian), trans. and ed. Rosella Mamoli Zorzi (Venice: Supernova, 2007). "Lure" first appeared in *Lure/Mamac* (Nis, Serbia: Niski kulturni centar, 2012).

Thanks also go to the Institute for Advanced Study, University of Minnesota, Twin Cities (Director, Ann Waltner), for a Visiting Research Fellowship in Spring 2006, during a difficult time, which allowed me to make substantial progress on this collection, and to the Stadler Poetry Center, Bucknell University (Director, Shara McCallum) for two summer residences. At the University of New Orleans, thanks also to the late John Cooke, to Peter Schock, and to the Office of Research and Sponsored Programs, especially Dean Robert Cashner, for released time and for their support. Individuals to whom I owe a deep debt of gratitude for support and advice include Donald Anderson, Richard Berengarten, Mary de Rachewiltz, Dana Gioia, Alan Golding, Cynthia Hogue, Bill Lavender, Hank Lazer, Svetlana Nedeljkov, Shelley Puhak, the late Lorenzo Thomas, Sonny Williams, Lee Zimmerman, and my wife, Biljana Obradović.

Table of Contents

Hamlet. Come for the third, Laertes. You do but dally.
I pray you pass with your best violence;
I am sure you make a wanton of me.

Laertes. Say you so? Come on. [*They play*].

Osric. Nothing neither way.

Laertes. Have at you now!

Hamlet V. ii.298-303

Clearance

The thing about an empty page is
not the neatness of it, nor its play

to memory, nor the pleasure it gives
being turned, nor its lack of an illustration

to distract my inattention there,
no matter how I may console myself

thinking so, as in gazing at a distant peak
I don't have to climb. Nor the luxury,

even, of someone somewhere managing
to throw all this space away

for nothing. Is it perfume from a dress
hanging idly in her closet? Or is it

the runway an airplane ascends from
after a loved one's departure, when I,

dangling by the large plate glass inside
the terminal, imagine the press of her flesh

just gone, quickly dissipating,
stretched out before me, unnoteworthy,

like gold to airy thinness beat,
like the hours I have left

I will never share with anyone
so eventually will forget, stark,

burgeoning, beautiful yet spare,

about to be laid bare, as I veer away

to return to old habits
newly strange to me now?

I. Bad Dreams

To a Friend Dying of Cancer in a War Zone

29 March 1999

Fatigue—a word in English meaning more
than *tired* or *exhausted*. Last summer your
impassioned heart, Drago, your energy,
unsettled me like sudden electricity,
a jolt of love ten times the strength of men.
Tonight I'm searching for that love again.

Summit Summary

Tactfully irrelevant as the strategic plan
tucked in the vest pocket of the colonel,
third from left, beside the female translator
in this wire photo of the president's parlor
equipped with Queen Anne couches and tables
during his meeting with foreign ministers
newly arrived from the north and west by
special convoy, under the protection of arms,
to discuss the latest peace proposal both sides
with the predictability of a boomerang
will later reject, I continue my work here
as, if not Melville's sub-sub-librarian over-
flowing with scholarly ambition but utterly
forgotten behind his moldy stacks, a poet
a little less academic than an argument
on the relative market value in autumn
of the butterwort between two carpenters
assessing the property of a modest house
whose blueprint has yet to be drawn up
on a tract near the town center next to
the bank about to implode under pressure
from the mistargeted bomb now en route
aboard the previously programmed missile
launched, as it turns out, just before these
same well-dressed dignitaries in this photo
completed their lunch of beefsteak and peppers.

The Secret of Stealth

for Adam Puslojić

What I don't understand somehow
about the obscene pun on "Big Mac"
we saw scribbled across the U.S.
Embassy wall in Belgrade—*Vi imate
mek, a mi tvrd*—something to do with
the flaccid penis Serbs think of as
America, applies, too, to those bombers
tooling invisibly through an empty sky,
those black hawks we praise as heroic
in their remove. It's like the guy
who charms the pants off the ladies
but never pulls his own zipper down:
Whom are we fooling by sending them?

We are not at war with a faceless enemy
down there, hacking children apart
cool as you please, caught red-handed
in our blue sights, digitally targeted,
but with ourselves, too moot to die
readily anymore for anything
or anyone. Imagine the tiny cell
we want to impregnate everyone
everywhere with. Imagine getting
trapped there ourselves, tucked snugly
inside, as though locked in the cargo bay
on a slave ship. Imagine hard love (*tvrd!*)
within that tight berth. It's no wonder

our bombardiers can't wait to get home.
Traveling concealed, even in the dark,
has its liabilities. But to be hidden
in America is to be stolid and manly

as apple pie, the one jammed in the pantry
between the beets and lard. No weapon
in your hands, or cradled on your lap,
is ever quite so big as when, unseen
on its rack, untouched beneath your stiff,
shiny belly, it promises to spread its cluster
of apple seeds, driven like pure snow
onto those flailing below, the same ones
otherwise sure to ruin your best laid plans.

Grief

offers no comparisons and teaches no lessons.
It sits across from you in this dark room
or passes by on the street, and if you should

lean toward it or attempt to exchange
a word or two, slowly it will maneuver
out of your way, its back turned

as though it hasn't noticed you. You try
but can never pick it out in a crowd
down at the station house, although someone

you hardly know, maybe met only once,
keeps coming into your mind, causing you
to question why you seem so unlike

yourself, like nothing else you can
remember: You forget to seek relief
in the usual ways, a glass of water

or evening light. Even stranger,
you imagine returning from an errand
or brief sleep, only to find grief

in a new hat parked on your doorstep
with a basket of fresh figs! It doesn't
matter, really, that it has a name, too,

that can be spelled out on a sheet of paper,
then erased, as haply as I,
the one typing this meek escape.

In *Travesty*

In *Travesty*, a novel by John Hawkes,
the Papa drives his wife, son and son's wife
toward a cliff (in France, next to a sea,
I think) to crash and die. Everyone balks,
learning how little Papa values life,
that he would ravage not only these three

who mean the world to him, but their love, too,
the trust they've put in him, letting him drive them,
for instance. Why would any man decide,
late in his life, living in France, to do
such a criminal act? How dare deprive them,
his loved ones, of their best years? Is it pride,

self-hatred, or ambition, this disdain
Papa has for those likely to survive him?
Does he fear how much his heirs will forget
or how much they'll remember? Fear the pain
of losing love, or of losing to rivals
who'll get to see ten thousand more suns set

on Normandy, Lake Erie, or Caracas
than he will? I'm amazed how Hawkes can write
so I'll feel sorry for an abject killer,
even if I can't recall where his attack was
nor how his victims looked. But here, tonight,
in pitch-black, death could not feel any realer.

General Advice to the Generals

So much to be done
    away with, so little time
        to remember what,

instead, was to be
    concluded in the best way
        possible, possibly

now never. OK. Forget
    what, against our better
        judgment, we thought

to have done. Instead,
    do what, with so little
        time, can still be

undone, and
    for the rest just
        do without. OK? I

am asking you: *Instead of*
    what you concluded you had
        to do, for once,

now or never, is it not better
    not to go against
        what we thought

our possible judgment
    might be, with so
        little time

to do away with
    and so much more

to remember? Forget it,

OK? Just once, for
     the rest,
         be still.

Sunset on Kalemegdan

Belgrade, Serbia, October 2000

We finally walked up to the monument
    after seven days of madness—
of conversations, conflicts, coffees, contracts
resolved, at last, among the advocates
    for change—to taste the sadness

of Kalemegdan Park above the fog,
    an autumn fog before the freeze
really set in. New Belgrade to the west
lay stained in white, thick as the hotel drapes
    each morning you would ease

back from the window in our room when steam
    behind them from the radiator
sizzled for an hour. But you couldn't sweep
this haze away. Instead, we turned and gazed
    across the Sava, toward the faded tower

of the television building, charred, splintered,
    like script in Arabic,
its twisted steel antennae etched in black
spelling out the story of the "smart bombs"
    that had seared its roof. You picked

out, through the dense cold, Hotel Yugoslavia,
    its long low garden block that lines
the Danube to its north. "Bombed, too," you told me,
"not open yet, though it's been eighteen months,"
    then spoke of other signs

of desecration, disrepair and damage:
    graffiti on the busts

of old war heroes I then photographed
with you between them in your stylish hat—
    a blue bloom in a bed of rust!

the scattered bricks and litter on the fortress,
    and not far off, unseen,
the embassy where four more people had died,
victims not only of the beams that crushed them
    but of the last regime

that had survived so long by vaunting the dead,
    a sacred Serbian tradition
as cherished as the fields of Kosovo.
The crowd around us didn't seem to mind, though,
    so we began to listen

to them, the strolling couples chatting, girls
    in leather coats, their necks
and legs exposed despite the brisk air, boys
taunting the girls with mournful grins, one woman
    browsing an article on sex

while she rocked her baby, two men at chess
    surrounded by an aging team
of experts dressed in tattered sweaters, leaves
drifting among them, even as they waited
    for the next move. Tossed in this dream

we stopped our talk and looked back at the sun,
    a fireball in the mist
blotting the fog that settled over Belgrade
like a splotch of blood absorbed in cotton.
    It oozed bright pink at first,

then disappeared, as lost as we were in it
    before the onslaught of the dark.
At peace, and still in love, we poked our way

among the few small groups lingering still,
    loathe to exit the park

for Knez Mihailova, for Hotel Moscow,
    our last glimpse of this city,
not ancient, not yet new, suspended here
between two rivers and the fog, that somehow
    has lived through the scorn and pity,

the pressed palms of a tyrant and the soft
    caresses of a treacherous friend,
rusting, sizzling, even as it gives way
to the likes of you, a blue burst in bloom,
    a light in shadow at day's end.

English Is Dying

English is dying. We may laugh,
thinking that, like the sun, it will take
ten million years to shrivel into
a black ball smaller than your fist
before it disappears. We may draft
contingencies or dream of a Mars
where the imagination lingers on in
frozen idioms, capsules of copulatives,
histories recording even the eyebrows
we now raise at those who question us.
We cannot even conceive of the death
of this music that stirs us to rise,
the words for strong thighs that cradle
our heads when, like me sometimes at home,
we crawl into bed to put wet lips beside
soft parts kindling sighs we claim
separate us from mere animals.

With so little time to recall what's said
in English worth repeating, we may,
like me sometimes downtown, run afoul
of nouns, mixing memory and lexicons
in a suture we want no truck with,
as we strain to graft what we know,
or think we know, thinking we know
something no one has spoken yet. Or
look to escape what diminishes us
en masse, until we are old enough
to know better but are no better off
for knowing. We may stash letters
from those we have come to love
for their beauty or grace, no matter
how broken, feeding our drive to make
these things last. But English is dying,

so to keep what we prize from oblivion
we must devise a future we need
to believe in as just the same, like me
with you sometimes, inventing our past.

RE: Volition

How like the tedium of afterlife,
my sleeplessness, void of ideas, or hope
for revolutionizing humankind.

To sit up all night and resolve the strife
of Palestine—that would be something!—grope
like Kierkegaard, even, maybe to find

not truth, exactly, but something more, more...
what? More pungent? Like blueberries? Instead,
I stare through darkness toward the window ledge,

redundantly imagining the floor
where I might drop my feet beside the bed,
rise then, reach for the shade, lifting its edge

to greet the dawn, and say, *Have at you now!*
What good am I if I break, like a brick,
only when the ground under me shifts and strains?

Yet angrily to strike out would allow
too little time to think. Ah, that's the trick:
somehow to nurture without leaving stains.

II. Quintessence of Dust

Seepage

Under the water, silence.
In the air, silence.
Above the deserted streets, silence.
From the capital, silence.

Through the attic roofs not axed out,
out of mouths of the infants, empty with hunger,
below the crypts, sodden
and grazed, at the bottoms of highways,
near the corner groceries,
in the birds' nests, dangling now
over stagnant pools, silence.

Silence for the benefit of the others:
For the yellow-smocked men and women, tacked
by exhaustion, drained of their brains,
behind the shadows left by the high winds,
inside the kitchens, dark with stench,
outside the long rows of busses, rusting,
within the laboratories, within the microbes,
surrounding the still cat, curled on the deck
next to the drain spout, its fur curdled from mercury
absorbed in the water,

absorbed in the water,
under the air where anxious onlookers, edging
toward the borders, crowd the brown basins,
where not a breath of moisture stirs
now, not the cusp of ease, not a camellia,
not a live oak unblemished,

silence.

And still from the capital,

Return to the Scene of

When is the next great fear?
Where is the next bright city?
What am I doing here,
inept at expressing pity?

The dead return to taunt
how I can't spell their names.
They lie across my lawn
like linen soaked with stains—

my doing, in other words,
my own death blotched in theirs.
I measure out in thirds
the gray dread in their stares.

Work crews x'ed exactly
where bodies lay washed down.
Forget what grief attacked me,
what green shoots shriveled brown,

what poison plugged my veins
the moment I arrived.
Instead, euphoria reigns
among those who've survived

(supposedly intact
like pupae sealed in wax).
I guess I'm glad I'm back.
Still, I can't help but ask,

Where is the next great fear?
When is the next bright city?
What do I do next here,
beyond expressing pity?

My Flock of Angels

O how I am grateful to the highway inspectors
who keep the bridges beneath from collapsing
like the house of cards that comprises our current
government! How I wish to thank those brave souls
in the city health department, the ones so willing
to run a gloved finger over the toilet seat
at my favorite restaurant—and the guys who ride
up and down, up and down, the elevators
in the tax department building downtown, risking
that the cables might snap, just to be sure I pay
my way as others have paid before me. Thanks to the
      vets
who readily look down the throats of rabid dogs or,
if necessary, squeeze a snake's neck or a cow's tits
for the safety of us all. Where would I be today
without the women who approved of my dress shirts
long before I ever dreamed of wearing black
with a gold tie. I especially wish to thank No. 82.

And the city utility expert who came out to my house—
Was it just last week?—to save my family from the gas
leaking from the gutter, odorlessly, or at least beyond
my ability to detect it, given my suicidal tendencies
in the past, my utter fascination with Anne Sexton, this
after we had had our house raised to meet the new codes
to spare us from further flooding, those dreaded, toxic,
      un-
godly waters that poured forth through our streets the
      last time,
unaffected by the millions we spent to guide them
elsewhere: My faith in him surpasses that which I have
in our new archbishop, or even in the Pope of my own
private, fairly inconspicuous cult. And speaking of
      martyrs,

I fall on my knees before the sanitation engineer, trash
collector, garbage man, recycler, whatever we call him,
who like Moses before the Israelites, gathering followers
at each crossroad, draws me to him when he passes,
as I wave my offering at him in its holy plastic sackcloth
carefully prepared from ointments of petroleum for just
this purpose, in factories spread throughout the Far East.

The taxi driver is my shepherd; I shall not list
the infinite sacrifices he has made to my convenience.
To Saint Meter Maid, who keeps my parking space open
or sheds her wrath on me if I trespass against her, may
she remember me kindly. The air traffic controller,
that chatty fellow who talks all aircraft down, not God,
is my co-pilot. And thanks to her who tests the DDT,
or whatever they call its successor now, safer or not,
that keeps the mosquitoes at arms' length from me.
Are those California tomatoes, faded in red and mushy
in the supermarket, safe now, Mr. Ginsberg? You bet!
If only we could say the same for casual sex. What the
        heck,
my heartfelt appreciation to that early wily Roman
who invented lambskin condoms, to the chemist at Dow
who ploughed through those tough years of harsh
unwarranted criticism by callous outsiders to discover
better bug bombs that won't poison most children
while looking for a cheaper way to sap sperm in the egg,

and to the National Guard in their steel-toed boots who,
for months after the disaster, trampled my neighborhood
to keep intruders off my lawn, to the social workers
        who,
out of deep respect for my privacy, have never asked me
anything about my personal beliefs, thus sparing my
        spirit
embarrassment, even as they dismiss my depression
as only temporary. Thanks to my local assessor, dear sir,

for continuing to assume my house remains in shambles,
and to those poor servants of the telephone and
    telegraph,
that host of outsourced, upstanding speakers of English
who battle Mumbai traffic each day on my behalf,
then wait patiently for me to finish punching the thirty
(or forty) numbers it takes to reach them alive, to hear
their glorious voices in a chorus Handel would envy,
who always ask me quietly to assure them they have met
all my needs, answered *all* my questions—*What's this
"universal fee," anyway? Does God exist? Am I guilty
of misreading the small print?* Forgive my ignorance
of acronyms and doxologies.
                              And though I may tread
the valley of the shadow of dread, most of all, most
of all, I owe my very life to you, you whom I don't
    know,
you who know nothing whatsoever about me and could
care less, who curse and bless my privacy yet,
    screaming,
keep me thrust in a world that will not leave me alone.
You aren't listening to this. You aren't peeking through
my window. You won't notice my obituary. You,
the one I most fear but may never encounter,
you who may as well save this world as ruin it, you
who have all the characteristics of a god, save
godliness, who keep to the billions I can't fathom,
your work and indolence hover above me daily
like the mosquitoes, flies, locusts, termites and flying
roaches that guide my journey through this sanctum,
otherwise mistaken as burgeoning with beauty and
    shame.

Disaster

A disaster is not a disease, nor
a bad habit, although a disease can be
both a disaster and a bad habit,
and a bad habit usually benefits someone,
a drug merchant, say. But a disaster,
come to think of it, sweeps through us

like a major argument in metaphysics, one
we can't change, try as we might. It's
as though the lines that depict the beloved
in, say, *Hylas and the Nymphs*, actually fit her
or him, not just the painter's imagination.
It's like those bad habits we prefer to,
if we can, overlook—or come to think

we might change, until we become obsessed
with thoughts of changes that cannot, will
not, come about. What sweeps through us,
whether from an argument or a disaster,
deposits itself in corners and under foliage
like toxic dust, stray pellets, or lust,
benefiting no one, but befitting everyone.

When Nadine Gordimer Spoke

When Nadine Gordimer spoke in New Orleans,
she lamented (it being May) the sensuous
landscapes of the veldt she found everywhere

in her earlier stories. Too many ideas
like plots of smooth suburban grass
laid over bulrushes or wild buttercups

had supplanted (now in her sixties) the brash
lines of passion that had once drawn saliva
from the back of her throat. The heavy

dark politics of South African strife,
having weighed on her for decades
like a heat wave that won't fade,

had made, she admitted, impossible a life
of repose, of secluding one sad mood
to tease out its colors in neat phrases

afloat on a novel's pages, in clusters,
like lily pads on a Japanese pond. Repression
(my word) encodes its own bond with you,

she added, which white Americans do not yet
understand.
                    Her eyes
intensely blue, her body frailer,

it seemed, than in her dust jacket photographs,
she dazed us with her rage for the orderly,
her spate of laughs, her worries

about failure. Later, when we touched hands,

as I was suggesting a plan for her family's
last meal at a New Orleans restaurant

called the Upperline, I, too, became hungry
for the days when the wisp of fingers
through my hair, or a friend's embrace,

brought me nearer a state of grace.
But such unspeakable harm has come
to so many, I fear nothing I trace

can justify these clear sounds I care
so much for (that gull's cry just now,
the fall of an off-rhyme like sex

after you expect it, the cooling voices
that charm me still the same way
Gordimer's did). I should shrink less,

I know, from distress at cruelties
I perpetuate myself whenever I wish
for the same lush landscapes of flesh

and native texture she spoke of, work
harder for peace.
                        Yet so long
as I can remember the fresh taste

of the sautéed redfish I recommended
that evening, or her words of sweet
regret, what use to measure our losses

together, atrocities no poet recalls
so well that we recoil for good,
if we can't also treasure the brush

of a palm, a footpath to school by a kraal,

the odd look a shaggy dog gave once
across a cornfield, that worn-down feeling

after you've spent a night caressing
someone ill who deserves your love,
or dressing up for a lingering meal

with no one especially important—these
the ideas lurking in books people write
for God knows what purpose they serve?

Grace

who sits in the booth
at the airport parking lot—
long term—and collects

from me, after my return
through the parting clouds,
like the gowns of angels

falling, my stamped
ticket and cash,
and who, before I am

released to the highway,
issues me a thin wafer
with her name and a round

smile on it, saying, *Keep this.*
This is your receipt. Have
a safe trip home, has had

so little bearing on
why I left here to begin
with, on the air traffic

control, on the words
I went there to hear,
that it shocks me to think,

weeks later, of her, her
black-rimmed glasses,
her bleak, Greek face.

In Our Time

In our time we needed no walls
to protect us from our enemies, not
because our enemies had no ladders,
as they'd had in earlier times, nor
because we had finally made peace,
but because walls, as we built them,
consisted of only water and earth,
so soon would crumble. In our time
our enemies came to believe in us

and fear us, both, as though they knew
we knew our strengths were justified.
In our time, our enemies, no matter
how carefully they tried to avoid us,
could be found everywhere—at least
by us. In fact, whenever we traced them,
we could defeat our enemies each time
we found even one of them wanting
so in these acts defeated ourselves. This

was not new, but in our time we became
the ones anxious to expose our enemies
as everyone else's enemies, looking away
from ourselves, always looking
away from ourselves. In our time,
water and earth were plentiful
and cheap, almost as plentiful, in fact,
as our enemies. We stood still only
when no one else was paying attention.

In our time, we worshipped the money
we printed with the tenderness of love,
not because we intended to oppress
those who refused to oppose our enemies

and devote themselves to our searching,
nor because our money was beautiful,
but because our money began to disappear,
replaced by the phantom of money
in which we believed but which soon,
no matter how carefully we traced it,

we came to fear—a phantom of a love
we sensed we should never question,
despite its sweet scent, not as an idol,
really, but more as a living god we
hastily yet faithfully, in our earnest
desire to suppress all our known
enemies, even those we need not
defend ourselves from, had devised
as the justifier of all the unjust-
ified things we wanted to be done.

We needed no walls, we needed no
enemies, and we most of all needed
no more money, really. We hardly
needed water and earth, looking away,
always away from ourselves. We had
our phantom, for which we stood still,
but we had no ladders for climbing
so defeated ourselves while no one else
was paying attention, and not long
after that, we crumbled.

Enough, Enough

Not willingly but quickly
we fled the dreaded scene. Fresh
the feeling. Clear the motive.
Like children from a prickly
possum, the moment they press
Danger, we rushed remote. I've

tasted water sweeter than air,
immersed myself in someone's hair,
stepped on a needle. I've swiped
a dollar without a care
for whom I've deprived. Don't stare;
you've done as much. The slate wiped

clean, that's what I think I mean
here. Concentration pure. No
lesson left behind to plague
mere experience. To have seen
enough, enough, let it go,
and then succumb to the ache...

Too easy to be a part
of history like this. Pray
it doesn't happen to you.
It requires no special art
nor grace, just being in the way,
since it doesn't matter who.

For Biljana, Who Says the Older She Grows, the Less She Knows

We dip in and out of knowing, the way, say,
without knowing, Petar puts his hands under water—
to cleanse, perhaps, but more to bring the sink

into his perception: His small fingers bow, separate
then spread. Through the clear stream he sees,
it seems, how the backs of hands cannot fold

upward, so he turns his palms around, in wonder
at their sudden magic, their slow curl and wrinkle,
the glaze that raises the red on his skin. With soap

now, he will soon twist both hands the other way
down again, rolling his wrists, all the while
talking himself through this (what we two

would have thought a) simple precise gleaming.
Can you and I offer each other what we know
like this? With little time left to lift our bigger hands,

breaking bread, or yours with a serving spoon, mine
holding Petar up toward the ceiling, toward the light
not of the sun, but of its glare through the glass door,

we can't measure well the silence growing in us, hour
by hour. Still, might we not use these same hands
to warm each other in the long season to come?

III. Bestial Oblivion

Lag Time

Forever in between
appointments I am missing and
the ones I'm waiting for—
too little read, too often seen,
without ideas or planned
unknowns—I linger by the kitchen door

fingering a small book's pages
as though I had an hour to kill
when I have murdered years
already, years, and latched in cages
the rabbits of my will
to run amuck, fearful of what appears

running amuck. I'm late,
as usual. My rabbits fidget,
like dancing drops of water
on a stove, and then evaporate:
no caterwauling, since it
would take all afternoon to reconnoiter,

but just the calm I crave
cut loose from assignation. Clear,
contained as well-wrought prose
yet fraught with ease, the thoughts I have,
loitering like this, never decompose,
suspended in a time that isn't here.

The Obvious

                        hangs
like a peach, over-
ripe, there before you,
untouched by birds,
avoided by rodents.

Why won't you pluck it?
Instead, you duck to
one side to avert
its scent, syrup-heavy
like late summer, and reach

toward a higher branch,
partially obstructed, your
fingers long, stretched
like the winding vines
of grapes you wish you

wore, bracelets trailing up
your arms. Instead,
you leave the peach
to lonely worms or flies
too busy to notice

the fear in your eyes.
I wish I could surprise
her somehow with
a richer peach, small
and tart, but I'm not

anywhere near this tree,
in fact, here behind
the baseboards, back
in the farmhouse, making

instead a study of fresh fruit

in a bowl. Nothing seems
farther from the truth.
Why don't I just pluck it,
arms' length and pungent?
No need to hide anymore.

Bestial Oblivion

Counting the days till you arrive
in white and black, or cream,
to sweep me up like dust, I dream
in lust, sometimes contrive

my waking hours to pass unkempt
like wild flowers, or sing
the sun to set on everything
except what I exempt:

a you, a woman smooth and cool
to lie beside in wonder
or slide my burning body under,
hardening to a jewel.

If yearning grew from absence, then
bluntly, when most you were missed,
I'd boast my best at having kissed
your lips, your breasts, your skin,

but my desire's color blindness
obliterates that past.
I need you here. I need you fast
against me. Now. I'm mindless.

Sleep Be Not Proud

Sleep is not death's second self after all.
This I realized while dozing off one day
and misconstruing what forecasters say
about how summer shrivels into fall.
True, sleep dulls. Still, the few dreams I recall,
like raw meats, often spoil, whenever I prey
too rashly on them in conversation, the way
steak too rare can taste like a stockyard stall.

Waking, in fact, better conjures the dead.
Whatever hours I have left are unknown
to me, as favoring a broken bone
to a corpse must be. And this pervasive dread
(which disappears whenever I nod off) instead
of rendering death null as inert stone,
convinces me every day my body's thrown
together like a hastily made bed,

biding its time until it's messed up again
by love, illness, or grief. A weekend guest
at the country home of consciousness, I'm blessed
occasionally by lazy evenings spent
with cool drinks on my host's veranda, but when,
between times, I get homesick or depressed,
it's then I sense death's emptiness the best—
unless, like bliss, death undermines intent.

The Reach

The grasp suffers the dissatisfaction
of the last bite of a meal too delicious
to have been served — striped bass, halibut,

lamb stew. The pinch keeps records
like a scout on the trail, having to answer only
to its captain, memory, who waits

in silence, back at camp. The nod
exercises hard every day until it grows
breathless, unwilling to let itself go soft.

The shrug can never be located,
its number unlisted, forever changing
addresses and friends. Hands on hips,

by now disgusted at how things have gone,
refuse to take separate holidays. Deep
in pockets, meanwhile, the ungenerous dangle

and fidget, whispering to themselves at parties,
furtively — that is, until no one invites them
back again. The raised eyebrow writes books

few choose to read and even fewer buy,
despite wide consensus there is wisdom
therein. Who can trust a scratched head?

Ah, but the reach, sworn to an allegiance
freely pledged, overextending itself to please
even the least likely to agree, thrives

on the in-between, leading the drive to
instead, yet, handing out sweets

in the meantime to whomever it meets

along the way, it tends to impede
the very ones it bends over backwards
to nourish, encourage, or relieve.

Appeasement

O shame, where is thy blush?

Much weighs on my conscience this season, Walt
    Whitman.
I have more to answer for than your gods have granted
    me time
to enumerate. The world knows, as everyone near me
    knows,
what I mean. Small boys who fear growing into men of
    rancor,
as their fathers have shown them anger and hatred,
know what I mean. My neighbor who only speaks three
    or four hundred words
in English but who has lived on the same block where I
    live now
twenty-seven years, having come from Nicaragua,
    knows what I mean.
Even the man in the large steel vehicle tailgating me on
    the crowded avenue uptown,
the one whose lips I saw behind me silently forming the
    words, "   ,"
yesterday because I would not accelerate fast enough
for him, when the streetlight changed from red to green,
so he might speed forward to veer around my little car,
    but who knew,
as he swore damnation against me, shaking his head
back and forth in disgust, back and
forth, back
and forth, disgusted, though he had nowhere to get to,
after all, in such a hurry,
knows just what I mean. Yes, even he, who disguises his
    shame
in impatience, under the shaved head of a vastly superior
    genome
ready every moment to defend to the bitter end

those things he thinks he loves, knows exactly
what I mean.

I have death to answer for,

the deaths of countless others whose bodies stretch
        before mine, across this country
from the white dunes of Provincetown to the caves of
        Painted Rock to the streets of Tijuana,
bodies like those one dollar bills (a billion, as I
        remember, though who cares) measured, one by
        one, in the *World Book Encyclopedia* of my
        childhood, dollar bills which if linked
could pave the way from Manhattan corners to the
        barrios of Los Angeles, east to west, back and forth,
not once, from there to there (and here to here), but
        thirty-three
or more times! one dollar bills far smaller than human
        bodies laid out—the difference, I guess, being that it
        would take but 300 corpses, give or take a few,
to create a chain a mile long, so
times that by 33 (or 3300 or 33,000) and calculate whose
        idea it was in the first place
to slaughter so many.

And the ones who have starved to afford me my hot
        morning coffee, why do they
impose themselves, like crows in my garden, on my
        meditation? And the ones
under the microscope of history, examined to be
        understood not so they might live
long, productive lives but so others after them who will
        never know anything of them,
might in a later generation live long, productive lives?
        Who has chosen them either to die or
become human, worthy of regard, maybe even of love—
        despite their having disobeyed?

And why have I forsaken them?

And the fishermen and fisherwomen, whom I trust
      because of the seas they traverse,
must I wipe them, too, from the earth in my
      carelessness?
Like the Hebrew women, the women of ancient Greece,
      Hindu women, women of the Sudan,
Amazons or Aztecs, those of the Aleutian Islands,
      Laplander women, women of Tibet,
of Texas before it gave itself to oil, women in Celtic
      cults, or those who knew those who knew
how it was to die in Jonestown in 1979, Malaysian
      seamstresses, New Orleans prostitutes,
I should wail, do nothing but wail, for these many dead,
      these empty faces and bodies not
bloodied but drained of their blood, sucked dry like
      buffalo skins stretched over stone
long after rain has evaporated and the ants and maggots
      have had their way, wail
for the suffering I have initiated, for the history I have
      erased, for my ennui when one
undeserving of punishment is punished, for the wry
      smile I try to conceal
when the President of the United States, my president,
      lies with relish, about which

I do nothing:

I do nothing to reprove the lives of those to whom I will
      never say a word, do
nothing to spare those whom, I admit, I will never
      understand
but whose unspared lives shame and splatter my own,
do nothing to begin my own recovery from the long line,
      the gamut of terror

and cold-blooded crime of my earlier kind, whose
    character I have inherited, that long line at whose
    end
I stand, head hung, shoulders drooping, more from
    exhaustion than from humiliation,
do nothing to move around those larger than I am, to
    whom I am allied, who protect
my interests from my president's lies by their
    phlegmatic looks, their kindly eyes, the diligent,
    mechanical
forward motion of each muscular arm against the wheel
    we all turn. I do nothing
in the hiatus of days, months, years—between the wars
    we lay out
like highways, wars we perpetuate by our building more
    highways, wars we
export as though they were fuel for our highways,
    thousands of highways on which to lay out yet more
    corpses end to end—
to alleviate suffering or slice into the momentum toward
    the next war next door. I am too tired, or so I tell
    myself, and cannot resist all this rolling machinery
    (literal as well as
figurative) that finds victims as though they were there
    all along, outside itself, waiting,
nor are our occasional meetings—yours and mine, Walt
    Whitman—good
enough, since inevitably you have others, many others,
    to meet, while I do not but am shut
in, like an Emily, shut not inside a house but inside a
    state of indifference.

I can't imagine appeasement as anything less than
    undignified, disgraceful, sickly.
I can't imagine self-esteem in anything less than a dream
    of domination, a long, drawn-out
dream with everyone looking at me, looking *up* at me,

afraid of what they see,
of everyone looking *to* me to make their decisions for
  them, divide their spoils,
disburse their riches, desecrate their divine—all to make
  room for the new,
while others bear the costs, whatever their burden. I
  can't imagine a prolonged peace
without me as the broker, the one who carries both good
  and bad news
to the world's sorry survivors,

I can't imagine a future,

no matter how inevitable it is, in which I will no longer
  matter, barely a blip in the mind of,
at best, a few school children, a few battered books, a
  future without America
in front of everyone's mind, coming round the bend like
  Susannah on my knee,
a future without steel, without concrete avenues in it
  more potent than bread and water,
a future untested by bombs, uninhibited by brass bands
  and banners, unyielding
to my insistence that we play every game my way, even
  if I am not the best player,
unbounded by my stride.
I can't imagine peace without pride anymore than
  darkness without electric light to penetrate it,
or a kitchen without butter. I am trapped, not in
my garden but in a heavy frame, a steel snare, a snug
  self-satisfaction
I am not about to redesign because well, frankly, why
  would I, how could I?

I am already appeased.

I am unwilling to change, more pleased by my

president's lies than the prospect of my
    disappearing, becoming no more important than the
    trees
in this season—the trees, that is, that resupply
the oxygen I want. I cannot restore the people I have
    eradicated, cannot bring fresh air to the tribes
    defaced, villages sprayed by my fire, waters turned
    yellow from whatever I have exhaled. I cannot
    make beautiful
the dead and displaced, redeem them any better than
    doom them. I can only
make more room, more room, and even doing that I will
    want credit, to be noticed
in one, last, apocalyptic gasp as the great master ship
    going down, the best hope
adulterated, who takes everyone else down with me into
    the deep
to be dashed like Atlantis on the rocks beneath the
    waves.

Even my disappearance will be marked by my
    indiscretion, my iron-nosed, hardheaded,
thoughtless individualism. Oh, say, can you save me,
old friend, by recalling my few acts of kindness, how,
    once, I extended my hand
to a child collapsed in the grass by a hillside, so that
    child might rise
reaching for me, not out of fear or disgust for all I have
    done,
but to touch me, to embrace the spirit of things I once
    said I stood for,
regardless of the trail of failure and lapse, a child who
    may sift, separate and see,
remember and proceed, holding a tuft of grass toward
    me in a gesture of peace,
not appeasement?

Hesitation

After a Poetry Reading, Delmore Schwartz Returns to His Hotel

That moment I walked in I lost my beauty.
And in a bookshop, no less! Everyone—
from grandparents and aunts I'd only glimpsed
above my crib, to that waitress with "Judy"
embossed across her breast who'd made a pun
on *just dessert* at lunch—flashed by like hints

from some Talmudic commentary. Barely
composed, and wobbling, I tried to grin
to mask that I could feel my bowels cutting loose.
The boy behind the register then snared me
and asked if I'd be reading "Gunga Din,"
a poem he'd memorized in school. "Obtuse,"

I muttered, "what I write." Fat books of verse
by poets I could not identify
marshaled the shelves, with me so lost among them
like Sherman at a powwow of Nez Perce,
my first impulse was to shoot. Who knows why.
Had I known any paeans I'd have sung one

to keep the drowsy store manager awake
as I mowed down "Biographies." Instead,
I fingered through *The Secret Life of Snails*,
feigning surprise, until my bellyache
devoured my insides. *I want to be dead,*
forgotten. Everything I think of pales

next to this bourbon bottle by the bed,
browner than Chief Joseph. I had "potential"
once. My ambition ranked me with the giants.
After tonight, my genius scalped and shred,

disgrace will seem about as consequential
as melting poetry down to a science.

This Latest Emptiness

This latest emptiness is not one
to lose sleep over nor drop tears
in your cups about, just because,
like the wooden sled we stored
summers outside in the shed
behind spider webs when I was a kid,
it has taken up a corner of the stall
so long
you can't imagine anymore

the quick thrill that later
will fill your small body
when you lunge downhill
before an admiring crowd of wool-
headed villagers stamping the snow
from their boots and clapping
their gloves to keep the cold air
at bay, while you slip by

like a jaywalker through traffic.

IV. As a Woodcock to Mine Own Springe

Lure

Very like a whale.

O, I would give up everything for you!
I would, were not the price you ask, a tad
more than I'm worth, fixed. So I wallow, too
cut off from whatever happiness I had

before I knew you to return, yet too poor
to sell out for a moment's ecstasy:
the whale unable, after he's washed ashore,
to flip himself and creep back to the sea,

beached in the air he needs to breathe, yet dying.
Who'd ever have thought, sharp as I am, that this,
this plight, would end with me as blubber sighing.
Yet I would give up everything for bliss—

I would, still at my age! Forget the sea.
I'd gladly suffocate, if you'd snatch me.

Country Matters: *Le Déjeuner sur L'herbe*

Sex for breakfast. The idea's scrofulous,
a thought *enfants terribles* toss about
till noon, while others calculate their profits
over coffee. Just one—one little kiss—
I thought, might douse that adolescent pout
of hers. Just one dab to her cheek (so soft it's

like peach skin, so easily bruised from poking)
surely would redden it. Such was my task
before we packed our picnic for the forest—
to plan so many variants in stroking
her hair and forehead, no one would dare ask
why she's naked. But like a grudging tourist

who hates having to shell out for a hotel
in the town where he grew up, I *had* to add
those two docile males, reclined, disengaged—
their knees lifted, arms stretched, both paunches
    swelling
from too much lunch, that limp switch, all a tad
debauched—as though the whole tableau were staged

to cloud my true design: My jealousy surpasses
even a salesman's for his wealthiest buyer.
This wanton life I celebrate shall never,
never!, be mine; the placid middle class is
too mired in carnal pleasures I aspire
not to devour me, haunting my endeavor

to bleed from myself the pure sublime in paint
until I die, or throw my easel away.

And yet, undressing her proves I'm just like them,
lurid yet sanctified, and quaint, so damn quaint!
The problem is that what I want to say
demands I somehow manage to incite them

without disrupting their dreams of her body.
Too bad admitting those who take no part
in art are art's best subjects—who use sex
not to be beautiful, not as a study
of the mystery of spirals, but to distort
their own conventionality—can't fix

what's wrong with me. What's wrong with me? I'm lazy,
and so detest armies and businessmen.
I'd sell my soul, I swear, for that thick peace
which passes disbelief. Of all the ways she,
while I'm observing her, holds herself in,
the one that most intrigues me is the least,

if I may put it this way, feminine.
Her lack of shyness I admire: Her thighs
she spreads like two greyhounds, claiming their space
on the too too solid grass. But her chin,
angled between her fingers in the guise
of some Salon art critic, bears a trace

of insolence. Her intellect, in fact, like mine,
falters the more she emphasizes it
the way too many brush strokes blur the action
they mean to flaunt. She hungers to define
herself for me, yet she disguises it
so brazenly, with such dissatisfaction,

her eyes (one rounder than the other) drown
behind that bored look her white skin absorbs
like dye in tincture. Our poor hearts are smaller
than brains in dinosaurs. Still, when we frown,

even shrewdly, we imagine it disturbs
the very air around us, like a midnight prowler

who hears each step he takes a thousand times
more loudly than his victims, upstairs sleeping.
But, unless we're fortunate, no one sees us
commit the most despicable of crimes,
harboring what we long for in safe-keeping
behind wide eyes. As if that could appease us.

Party Look

The look you gave across the room,
sensing I, too, had been looking at you,
interrupted that casual afternoon
    the way a door swings open two,

    three, or more times before you glimpse,
gasping, the body on the floor. I thought
little, at first. The faint smile on your lips
    dismissed me, hiding how distraught

    I later surmised you must have been—
assuming you became undone as I did,
smiling my way through plastic cups of gin.
    The few words we exchanged confided

    nothing, like most of what I've said
until now, so unless you find this you won't guess
what I've resolved: Just once, before I'm dead,
    in some small cove, I want to press

    myself against you more than once—
assuming you'll feel as unbound as I do.
At least then, even if we resort to grunts,
    you'll know I know you knew I eyed you.

To Gisela, Squatting

What is it about
the back of
your bare calf
pushing up into
the curved bottom

inside your thigh
that moves me so?
The thin dark streak
between each limb
like a compass needle

extending to your
knee, the groove
and shallow canal
between your raised
heel and full muscle

succulent still,
even at your age,
thirty-nine, hold
my eyes, as though
a leg folded over

itself told mysteries
or lies equally
well, and equally well
I follow
their fine topography,

my eyes drifting
south to your sea
of surprise, its gift
a mouth at the end
of the bend in the line.

A Rasputin of Emphasis

variations on a line by Frank O'Hara

Breezing Phidippidesily by my Le Corbusier,
"Feeling more Brancusi than usual?" she asked.

I was Eisensteined, John Locked in a lost Maeterlinck.
"So let's de Sade right here! Or Petain!" she
        Bismarcked,
DeGaulling Churchills of terror down my spine.

"Together? Now?" I Welked, alarmed as a camel,
as I T.E. Lawrenced, then D.H.'d, side to side,
not recovered yet from my inflamed Longinuses,
my throat still Horace, my voice as Xanthipped
as the sands of the Socrates Coast.

But with Ictinus fingers she Nietzsched my neck
in a tender Lenin of love, our whole afternoon
unHooverly spent in Whistlers of near misses
(her juicy Cassatts, the Werner Von Braun in my lap!)

until on the verge of a total Toscanini
in utter Disraeli and Gladstone,
she Carmen Mirandaed straight from my flat
and sped off in her Xavier Cugat.

I Li Po'd from my Corbu but last Galileoed her
Carl Saganing out of sight in a Wily Coyote of dust.

To have been Henry Clayed
by her George Frederick Handels
with none of that old Bach magic
to Byron off my Knute Rocknes!

Believe me, I was Percy Bysshed!

74

To have William Henry Harrisoned me
so Enola Gayly, and then to Foyt,
A.J.! I was Nikitaly Kruschevt!

So I Samuel Coleridged off to my bed, Fay Wraying,
"Mishima me! I've been Sylvia Plathered!
She's Idi Amined my Amelia Earhart," I cried,
in deep Jimmy Hoffas and Calvin Klein pants,

"To Nathan Hale with her! To Trollope off
so unGrace Kelly. She should be Nabokov of herself!
Tchaikovsky her! Franz Kafka her!
I'll Judas her! I'll Iago her, in fact!"

Things like that.

Not one to Liebniz my words, though,
pacing in a Sousa of steam, entirely Pasternaked,
I Genghis Khanned whatever I Kubla'd of my poor
        Marco Polo,
hanging my limp Teiresias over my porcelain green St.
        Joan,
more Sitting Bull than Balanchine,

when amid this utter Confucius
I'd Pizarroed myself into,
in a Kandinsky of color it came to me,
yea, even Giuseppe Verdier!—a Juan Miro on my soul—

to Johann Wolfgang her von Goethely
might better Milhous Nixon her Eleanor of Aquitaine,
might render all the more Edmund unHilary
the glorious Mountbatten of her attack.

Thus Custerly, in a Gandhi of magnitude,
I Spinoza'd a little, Kerouacked a cab,
then Melvilled downtown, where, flushed

in a Millard Fillmore of expectation,

I Patty Hearsted a Schoenburg of bystanders,
Scarlatting them unPetroniusly, John Wayned
Hannibalistically to a nearby Edward Teller booth,
where I Salvador Dalied a number
I Picassoed at random, and Ezra Pounded
(rePindaring in moaning Yeatses and Nerudas),

"Oh, Bosch! You Immanuel Kant
Empedocles me that way
and expect to Hegel away with it Dred Scot!
Dante Alighieri me again, you hear?
or I'll Grigori Rasputin you back."

Your Other Woman

That woman who exposed her breasts to me
was not the one you prophesied.
Exactly as you'd said, she suddenly
undid her blouse and pulled the front aside,

inviting me under those evergreens
to taste her chalky, freckled flesh
and press my palm inside her open jeans.
I hesitated, trying to refresh

my memory of what else you'd predicted:
Reclined against a tree, yet tense,
she'd guide me to one breast, you'd said. (I licked it,
conspiring with my silence.) In one sense

she matched your dream of my desiring—
nudging me down between her thighs
where, coaxed by her sighs, my mouth searched the
        spring
my tongue drew moisture from. Her muffled cries

as you'd imagined them, garbled the words
she seemed determined not to keep,
words voiced as sounds shaped to be overheard,
as though like you she felt her body leap

some crevice, then savored the journey down.
You wouldn't have been disappointed,
had you stepped out, dropping the dressing gown
you'd loosened as you'd told me this, and joined us

enraptured by the woods, just how you'd promised
you would, with one hand on my back,
one fondling her cheek, while you two kissed

for the first time. You might have been distracted

by the pine smell, unmindful how her taste
felt different on your lips from mine.
You might have led her onto me and faced
the two of us entwined, tracing the line

from her to me, while I stared up at you
and she clung to your shoulder. Still,
nothing, nothing, that happened could subdue
the indescribably delicious thrill

I won't ever forget of lying at your side,
spent yet alert, breathlessly heaving,
listening to these things you prophesied,
seduced by all you then had me believing.

Flattery

is underrated and will often get you
everywhere. Like a satellite tracking system

it looks down on you, able to pinpoint
even the moles festering beneath your

slowly thinning hair, as it drifts
hundreds of miles above you, lingering,

patient as global warming. It has the slick eye
of the paid assassin, loyal to his boss,

who can pick you out of any grocery line
or college reunion catalogue. It knows

its limits yet is always ready to test yours,
with the lure of the puzzle no one can resist.

When it strikes, you may try, demurely,
to duck from its sway. Good luck, sucker.

But if you just let the professional do its job,
think of the compensations: Temporary ease

in which even the bone spurs on your spine
appear cute, the pleasure of knowing exactly

how much you are misunderstood, and occasionally
you even get a free drink—*mmm! Scotch!*

Never shake a stick at that! Leave virtue
to the anonymous. You'll join them soon enough.

And for now bask in the glow, radioactive,

if not radiant, that carries you through

the awful recognition that underneath it all
the company you keep you will keep

whether your story gets written or not.
Luck of the draw, really, so just take it,

that dart piercing your nape. It may stun you,
at first. It does smart—but for that salve, *mmm...*

indescribably delicious!

Poem ("Terrific this pale sun")

Terrific this pale sun
to oblige not with heat
but enough light to blend
the leafless trees with one
short-antlered deer, whose feet,
splayed slightly, freeze, pretend-

ing not to be spied on but,
despite being exposed,
to vanish instead, casually—
like your remark, when what
you said, just now, supposed-
ly pertained not to me

but to two we both know
who, nothing like us, drift
to where they don't belong,
then try holding still below
the breeze, not to be sniffed.
Ah! Beauty can be so wrong!

The Thought I Would Express

The thought I would express to her
    and only her,
sitting beside me quietly,
as though it never would occur
    to her that my thoughts blur,

escapes me in this hour alone
    when like a stone
I rest, mindless, improperly
and insignificantly prone,
    unseen, unheard, unknown,

with nothing to contribute to,
    nor see me through,
this present crisis pricelessly,
as elsewhere she, who has no clue,
    rises, becoming you.

V. A Congregation of Vapors

Part of a Sudden

Far be it that I should repine.
— Anne Bradstreet

I feel pretty
   good about myself
      some days, wearing
creased clothes low
   and tucked under
      my belt, although
the heat won't
   cease and my mood,
      I swear, veers

like thread off a
   spool, left then
      right, and I can't say
why or when, when
   nothing near to
      what some call death
interferes, but then
   it always does, one
      way or

another, flaring in me
   at night or, for
      that matter, where
ever I may
   try to cool my
      pelf, my pate,
so if I should say
   I am pleased,
      believe it before

it's too late, maybe
   three a.m. even and

again I'm
off in battle to
dispel this dread,
this flight fare-
well like a lightning
strike, my home
gone up in a blaze

like that.

Spring Offensive

So little cause for carolings...
— Thomas Hardy

The birds keep singing in the dark
as undeterred as Englishmen
in Africa; my neighbors quiet—
sound asleep—I lie here stark
and fast, near the millennium,

bewildered and as unconsoled
by all the things I thought I knew
as empires by their allies. Still,
this music fills my room, unspoiled
as though it were the one thing true
my country hasn't tried to kill

or bind into its vast regime.
If I, too, could only sing, instead
of tossing dumbly through the night—
anxious to exorcize this dream
and rest in peace in my own bed—
I might not dread the morning light,

dread finding out what new assault
was launched in darkness from the sky
against whomever's next in line
to be disposed of. So who's at fault,
then, these ecstatic birds, or I?
Cowering in my own design

of arrogance, hung up on the air,
I'm stuck, the victim of their song
(whether propaganda or prayer)
insisting nothing can go wrong,
and nothing I do can defy it.

Reading Philip Larkin at 3 AM

Only depression keeps me up this late
at fifty-one—not wine, not girls, not talk
even, as once it might, with friends I'd wait
hours for, as each decided on our walk,

usually through some poorly lit side street
or tree-lined park better attended to
than any place near here, to tell me sweet,
long-guarded secrets of love, or some taboo,

fearing I'd judge her or him less than sane,
when what most sidetracked me then was I might,
inadvertently, nod off, not remain
alert enough. Those days, the nub of night

burgeoned with mysteries, like passion fruit
(the name, not that mauve thing with its thick, gritty
    rind).
Now, reading Larkin, whom the day left mute
so only in the darkness would he find

his way around a language he could master,
I cherish being not asleep, though sleep,
I suspect, would help me think much faster
and probably not then get depressed. And keep-

ing hushed, I find this company of one
who, often lonely, drank too much and snapped
by sixty-three, dying miserably, fun;
more succulent still, his fruit, tart yet apt.

Done Reading

I doubt I'll read again
F. Scott Fitzgerald's *This Side
of Paradise*. I'm twenty
years older than he when
he wrote it so can't backslide
now and choose (among the plenty

of things I haven't read
by him) that book, because
as much as I might learn
from his mistakes, instead
of searching for his flaws
in my free time, I'll turn

to the mysterious
new moods I'll look to leap
from the just-published pages
of those the omnibus
reviews praise as our deep
contemporary sages.

It's sad to think that spring
I savored Fitzgerald's prose,
like an old friend I've lost touch with,
is gone for good. Books fling
secrets no friendship knows
across the body, flush with

discretion. And in that heat
of innocence undone,
age notwithstanding, I
invariably have felt complete
dissatisfaction. Still, one
by one, the titles high

atop my shelves disown
all claims to permanence,
like aging queens. *Prepare
to be forgot*, they groan,
even as they betray the sense
I'll always find them there.

Acceptance, Finally,

as when a street out of town
evens, narrows
      without warning
into a gentle right turn

neither of us anticipated, then
abruptly enters a dense fog,
      so we stop and
log hours of lying still on our

backs like two girls at the toe
of a tall pine, tugging at our wrists
      and tilting our knees
up until at last bare needles

high in the trees scribble
across the sky's clearing (we
      twist over each other
squinting to see) what one day

we will remember as, the
clouds now sweeping south, a surge
      of sheer delight:
our blue prize.

What Are Eyes for?

"Shedding" tears, as though
letting them drop meant
putting them in storage.
Whom should I despise

then? What are eyes for, dry,
but to see through whatever
they see and gauge from there
what to assess of what

lies beyond sight. We do,
in other words, cry a lot
for what we have lost
in order to identify

what remains, not what's
immortal, surely—grief
has taught me at least
that much,—nor holy,

since it arises from our
crust. Not lustful, either,
though the absolute pain
to me seems the same,

but a thing traced, like
blood, or an awfully
familiar name, unwittingly
unwilling to go away.

I weep to keep that
intact, in fact, don't
you? You think it may
be true? Well, I do, too.

On the Fly

Am I glad to discover I'm not
what I thought I was or, changing,
am I in fact nothing, like the skin
I shed every time I wash, soiled
matter, then, the thing I hold
most dear?
    I don't believe
what I said just now, but how
I said it, I am, you can imagine,
relieved to hear, managing
well enough. Yet is it me, after
what I say to myself, or
am I, in fact, now gone again,
tucked behind the quiet curtain
of an unenviable ignorance,

like the fly between the window
and closed blind, caught without
recourse, doomed, though a nuisance
all the same, even on its last
circle of seeing the bright world
it can never become a part of
still abuzz with all its possible lives,
alarmed at none of them but the one
now disappearing disappearing?

Miracoli

She counted the steps to the chancel, then slid
to one side, maybe to hide, maybe to emerge
from the stream of those who'd climbed before
and after, away from the gilded red runner newly
draped there and the sign, "No visitors beyond here."
Her fair hair, fallen to her shoulders, in the off-light
from the rafters, grew paler than heaven. No one knew
what language two worshippers spoke in one pew
while the others, like spry flowers in neat rows,
threw glances at the railings either side of the stairs,
the ivory-faced sirens beneath them abruptly aglow,
and above them the small figure flecked by the sky.

Before we withdrew, the scarf over her shoulders,
blue and red, slipped, though not indecorously,
exposing the delicate line of her neck. Only whispers,
of an indecipherable nature, broke from the nave,
cool as a cave, stark in spite of its speckled design.
Outside in the glimmer of day, after another moment,
she mentioned not the carvings we had entered to see,
nor the rose swirl in the green-gray marble I treasure,
but the unearthly music that had arisen from the choir,
no choir present, a music she must have suddenly
imagined, flooding that space where little air escapes:
It was silence I had sought, where she had found,
among the quiet parishioners, a fray of song.
I, who like to sing, pass on this memory, sprung
like a shout of sprigs in spring, from one now gone.

On the Poet

John Gery's previous books of poetry are *Charlemagne: A Song of Gestures* (Plumbers Ink, 1983), *The Enemies of Leisure* (Story Line, 1995), *American Ghost: Selected Poems* (English-Serbian, tr. Biljana Obradović, CCC, 1999), *Davenport's Version* (Portals, 2003), *A Gallery of Ghosts* (UNO Press, 2008), and *Lure* (English-Serbian, tr, Svetlana Nedeljkov and others, NKC, 2012), as well as two chapbooks. His other books include *Nuclear Annihilation and Contemporary American Poetry: Ways of Nothingness* (UP of Florida, 1996); the literary guidebook, *In Venice and the Veneto with Ezra Pound* (with Rosella Mamoli Zorzi, Massimo Bacigalupo, and Stefano Maria Casella, Supernova, 2007); *Hmayeak Shems: The Poetry of Pure Spirit* (with Vahe Baladouni, UPA, 2010); two edited collections of essays on Ezra Pound and on Imagism; and two edited anthologies of poetry. With Vahe Baladouni, he published *For the House of Torkom* (CCC, 1999), a translation of the prose poems of Armenian poet Hmayeak Shems. He has received, among other awards, a Creative Writing Fellowship from the National Endowment for the Arts, a Fulbright Fellowship to Serbia, a Research Fellowship at the Institute for Advanced Study, University of Minnesota, three Artist Fellowships from the Louisiana Division of the Arts, and the European Award of the Circle Franz Kafka, Prague. A Research Professor of English and Seraphia D. Leyda Teaching Fellow at the University of New Orleans, he directs the Ezra Pound Center for Literature, Brunnenburg, Italy. He lives in New Orleans with his wife, poet Biljana Obradović, and their son, Petar Gery.

CPSIA information can be obtained at www.ICGtesting.com
Printed in the USA
LVOW09s2128211114

414959LV00002B/5/P

9 781625 490704